Mel Bay Presents

Texas Fiddle Favorites for Mandolin

**By
Joe Carr**

Online Audio

To Access the Online Audio Go To:
www.melbay.com/98404BCDEB

ONLINE AUDIO

1	Red Apple Rag [2:07]	7	Bitter Creek [2:22]
2	Durang's Hornpipe [2:08]	8	Dusty Miller [1:50]
3	Tom and Jerry [4:14]	9	Twinkle Little Star [2:41]
4	Billy in the Lowground [2:20]	10	Sopping the Gravy [2:52]
5	Midnight on the Water [1:49]	11	Ace of Spades [2:49]
6	Jesse Polka [3:21]	12	Dill Pickle Rag [3:01]

1 2 3 4 5 6 7 8 9 0

Visit us on the Web at www.melbay.com — E-mail us at email@melbay.com

CONTENTS

INTRODUCTION

In this book/CD, Joe Carr presents his advanced mandolin arrangements of 12 well-known Texas-style tunes. The arrangements are inspired by the popular Texas contest fiddle style. The companion CD features all the tunes with full bluegrass band accompaniment. A volume of Alan Munde's banjo solos from the CD is also available.

Texas style fiddling has emerged this century as a unique and distinct regional fiddling style. It has also been the model for the modern contest style as exemplified by players including Mark O'Connor. Bluegrass fiddling was first influenced by the Texas style through eastern fiddlers such as Howdy Forrester whose performances were inspired by Texas fiddlers. Later, western fiddlers, including Oklahoman Byron Berline, directly influenced bluegrass music through performances and recordings with major bluegrass performers.

Through the years, a number of Texas-style fiddle tune arrangements have worked their way into the bluegrass repertoire. However, a number of great tunes which appear primarily in the Texas tradition have been overlooked by the bluegrass community. We hope to at least partially remedy this situation with this project.

The Texas fiddle style is characterized by (1) slower tempos than are typically found in Eastern styles; (2) more frequent use of the slur, triplet, and other forms of ornamentation; (3) fuller development of melodic themes; and (4) less rhythmic bowing patterns than are typically found in Eastern styles. It was our intent to represent these tunes (with only a few exceptions) in the melodic and rhythmic approach of the Texas fiddler. We are deeply indebted to Slim Richey for providing us with his own transcriptions.

Alan Munde and I discovered Southwestern fiddling early in our music careers. Before the bluegrass boom in Texas and Oklahoma in the 1970s, bluegrass pickers and events were few and far between. On the other hand, fiddling and fiddle contests have long been popular in this region. Alan spent many of his early years in music attending and playing at these fiddle events. This influence has always been evident in his music. Fiddle music presents unique problems to the banjo and Alan is known as one of the leading transcribers of fiddle music to the banjo. This album will only enhance his reputation.

My love/hate relationship with the fiddle began in the 1970s and has resulted in more sold or abandoned fiddles than contest trophies. My music on both the guitar and mandolin are heavily influenced by Texas fiddle music.

Our goal is to bring together two musics we love and to expose our bluegrass friends to the world of Texas fiddling in a familiar bluegrass music setting. We hope you enjoy it.

— Joe Carr

JOE CARR

Guitar players may not recognize Joe Carr's name at first, but his face is probably familiar. That's because he appears in more than 25 different instructional guitar videos ranging from county western swing, bluegrass, and even heavy metal! Add to these his videos on mandolin, fiddle, banjo, and ukulele and Joe may be the most recorded video music instructor anywhere.

Joe is a self-taught musician who started playing the guitar at age 13. "My guitar heroes were the stars of the sixties, especially the folk musicians," recalls Carr. "One day, a high school friend played a Doc Watson record for me and flatpicking became my life."

Joe must have learned his lessons well...a few years later he was hired to play guitar in Alan Munde's internationally known bluegrass group, Country Gazette. During the next six years Joe recorded three group albums, numerous sideman projects, and produced his own critically acclaimed solo guitar album, *Otter Nonsense.*

Joe left the Country Gazette in 1984 and joined the music faculty in the unique commercial music program at South Plains College in Levelland, Texas. Since then, he has worked with many talented guitarists including the late Chris Austin of Reba McEntire's group, Ron Block with Alison Krauss, and Heath Wright of Ricoche.

Joe continues to perform nationally in a duo with former Gazette leader and South Plains College colleague Alan Munde. "Alan and I have a great artistic communication that leads us into many new areas of music," Joe says. In addition to their recordings on Flying Fish Records, Joe and Alan co-wrote *Prairie Nights to Neon Lights; the Story of Country Music in West Texas* for the Texas Tech University Press.

Joe is a regular columnist for *Flatpicking Guitar Magazine* and *Mandolin Magazine.*

RED APPLE RAG

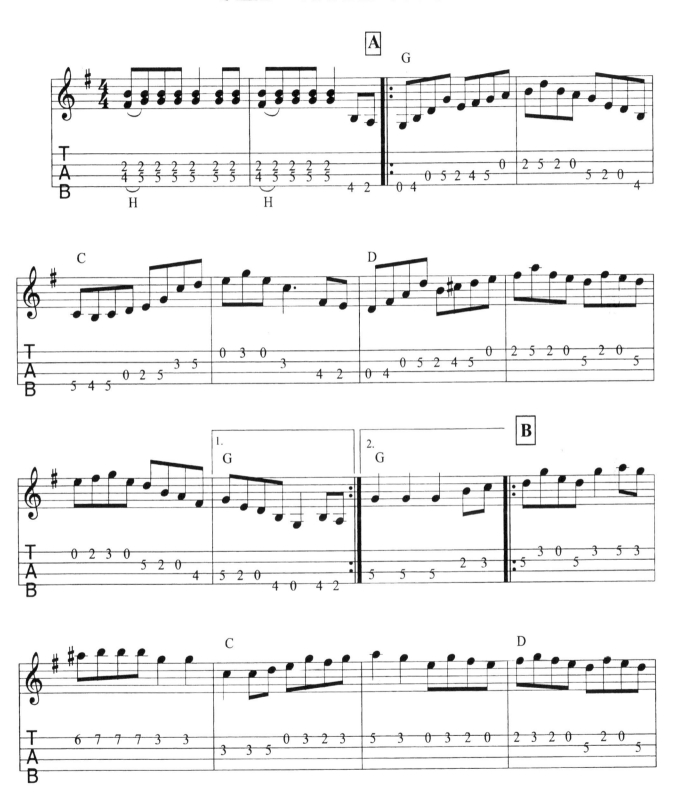

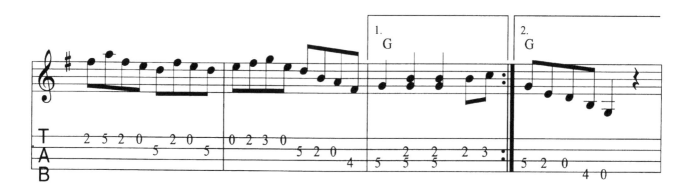

Banjo/Fiddle Solos

6

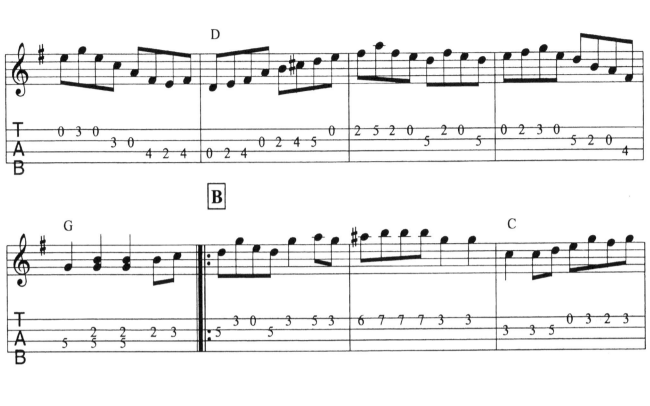

Durang's Hornpipe - Rhythm

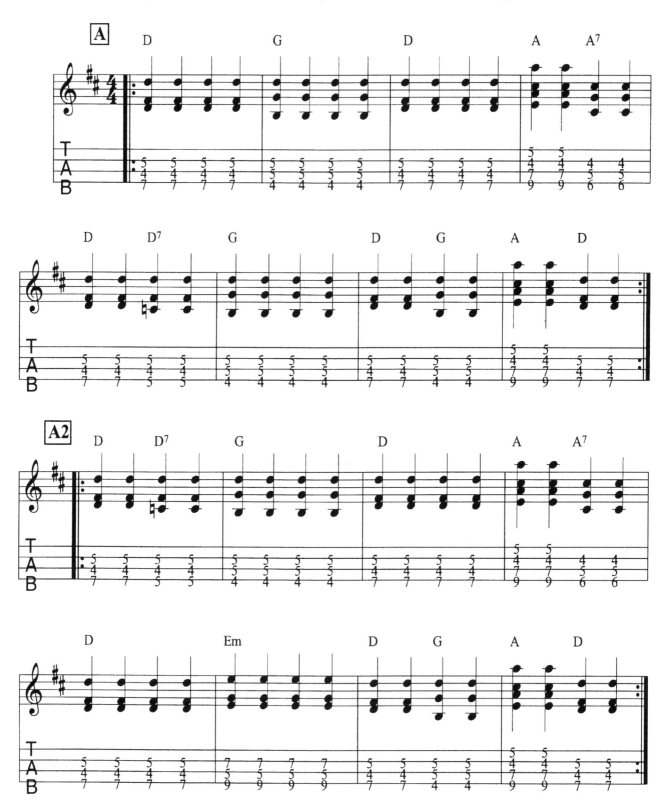

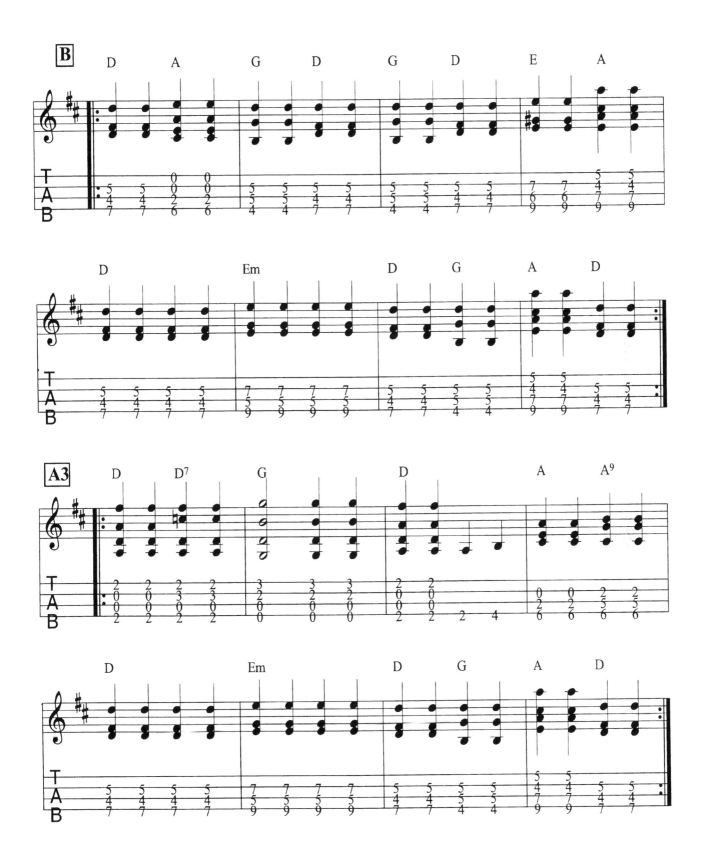

9

TOM AND JERRY

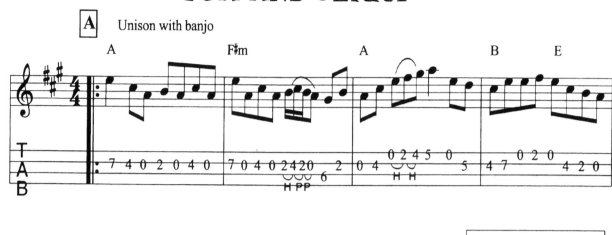

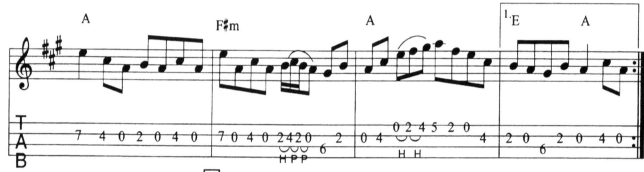

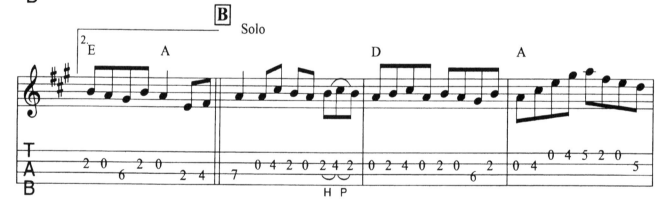

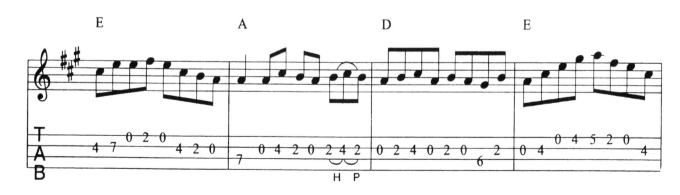

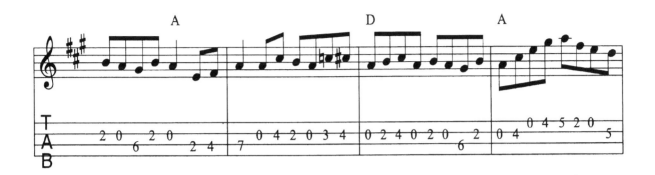

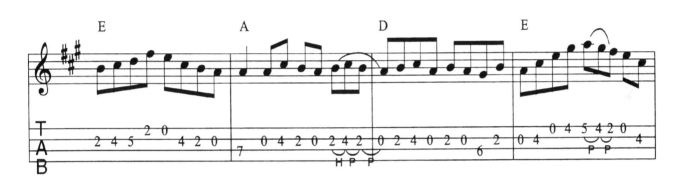

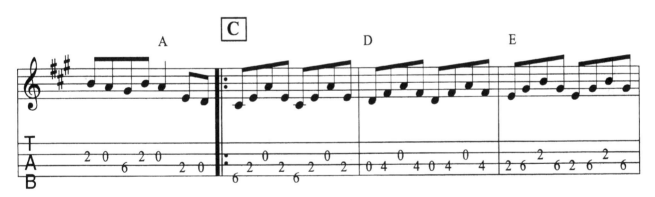

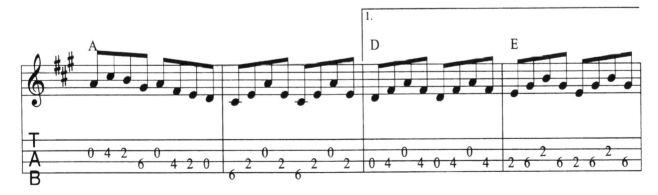

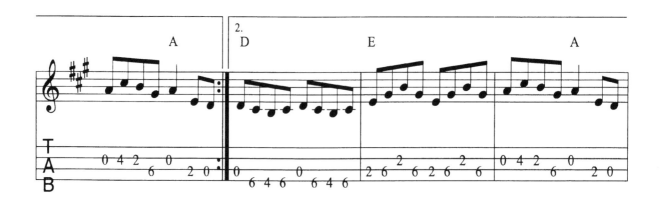

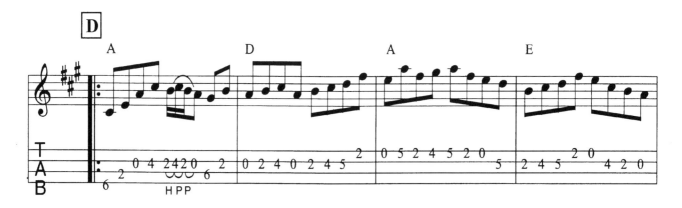

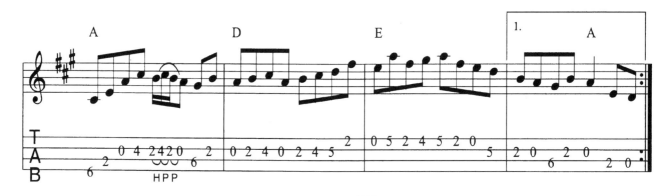

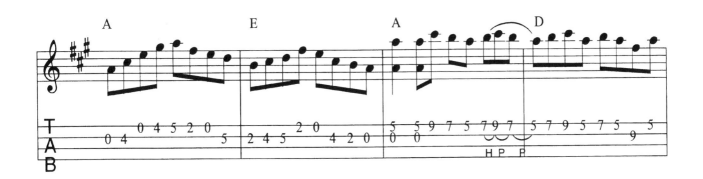

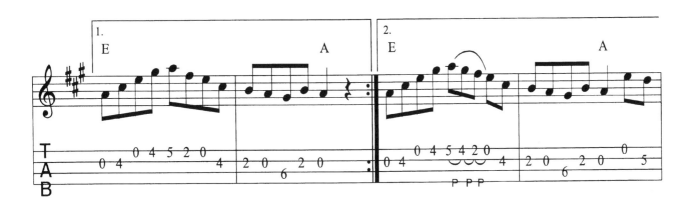

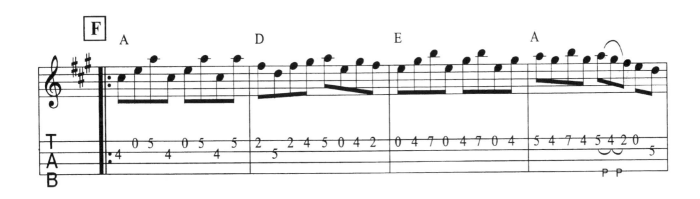

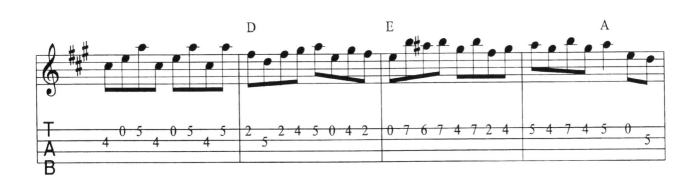

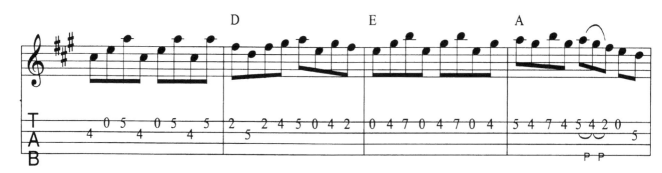

Repeat B & A

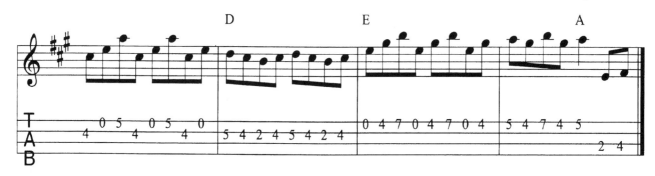

BILLY IN THE LOWGROUND

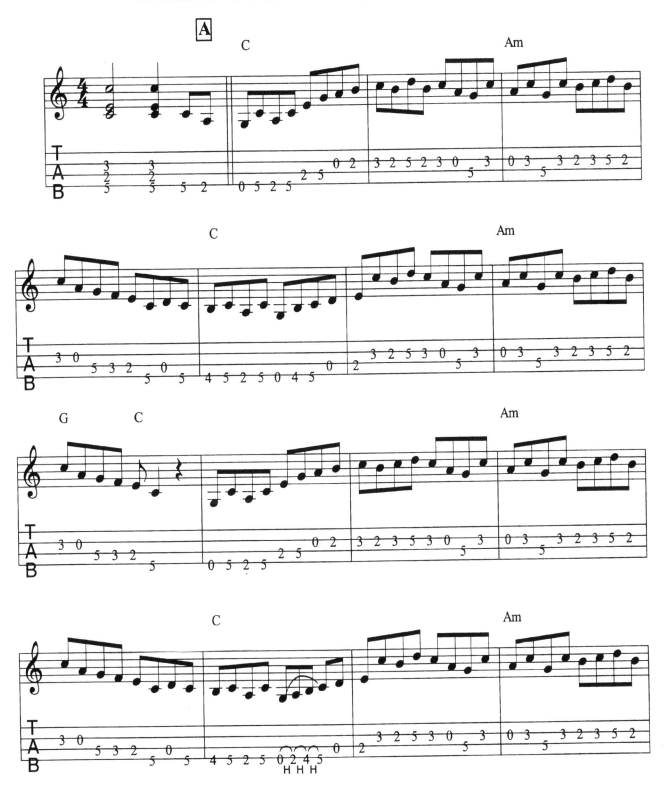

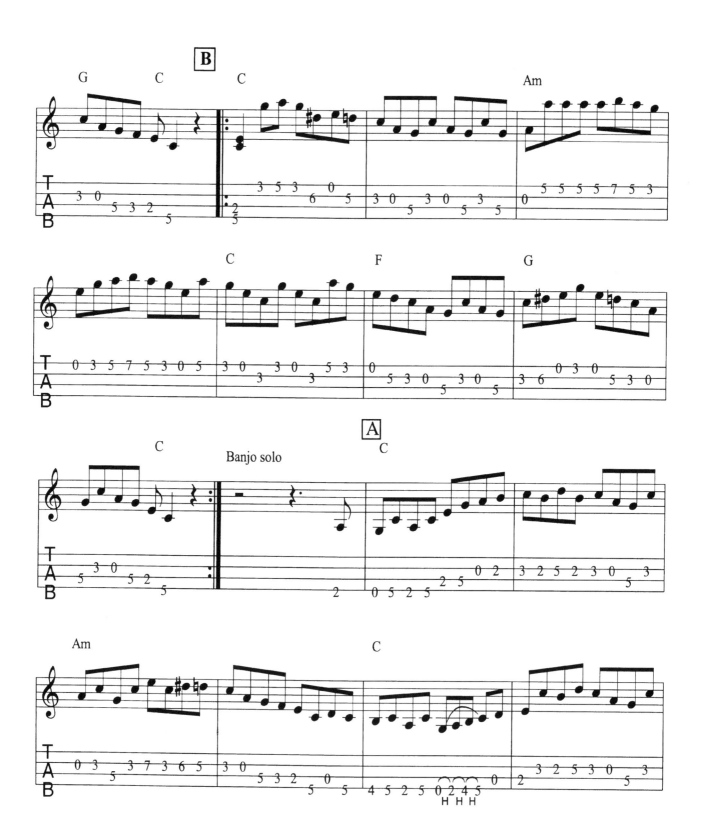

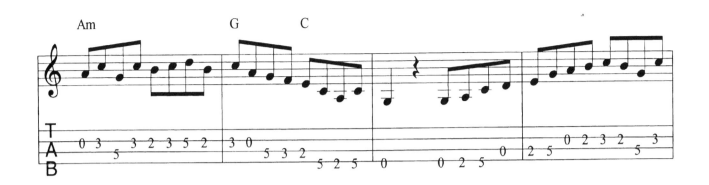

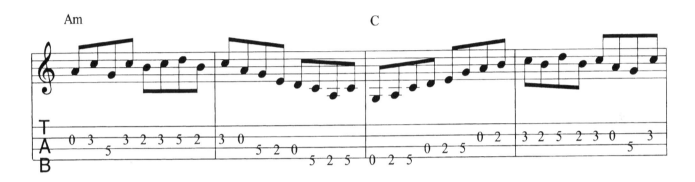

B

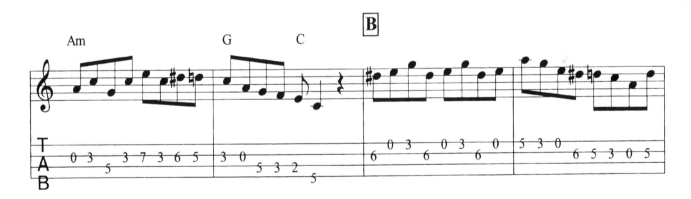

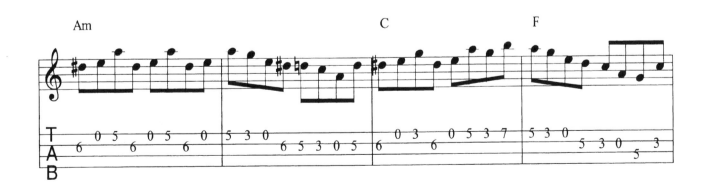

Banjo solo   Ending lick

This page has been left blank to avoid an awkward page turn.

MIDNIGHT ON THE WATER

Tuning D D A D, play as written

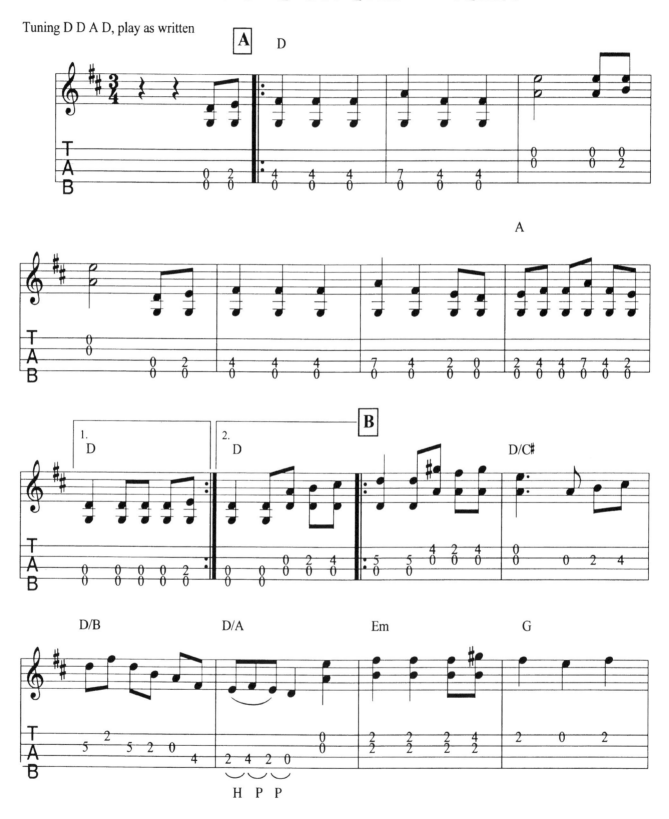

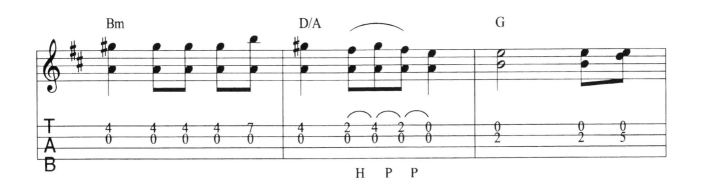

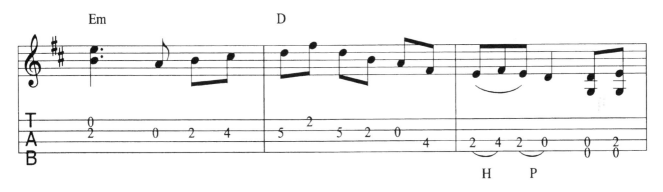

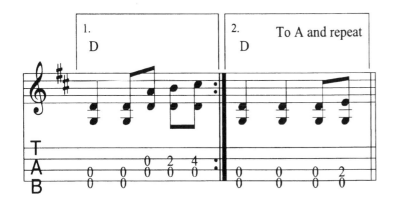

JESSE POLKA

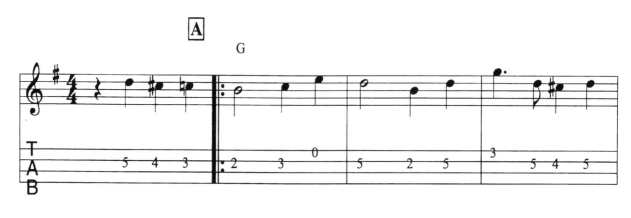

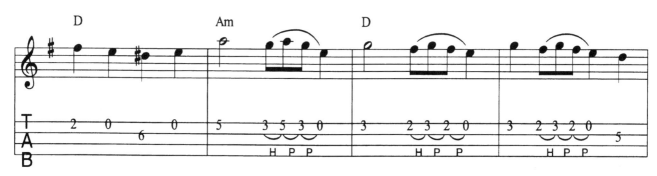

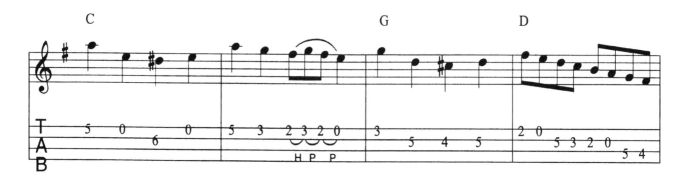

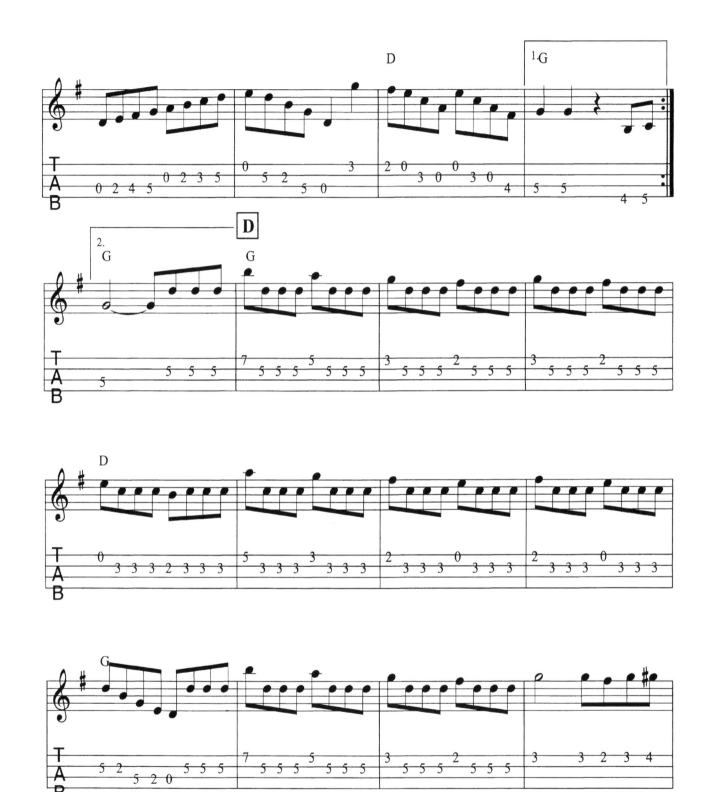

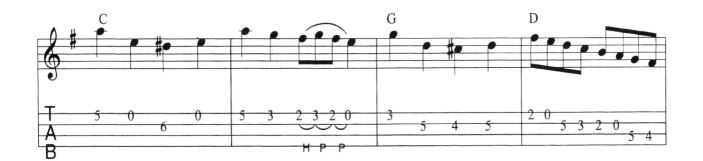

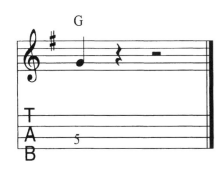

BITTER CREEK

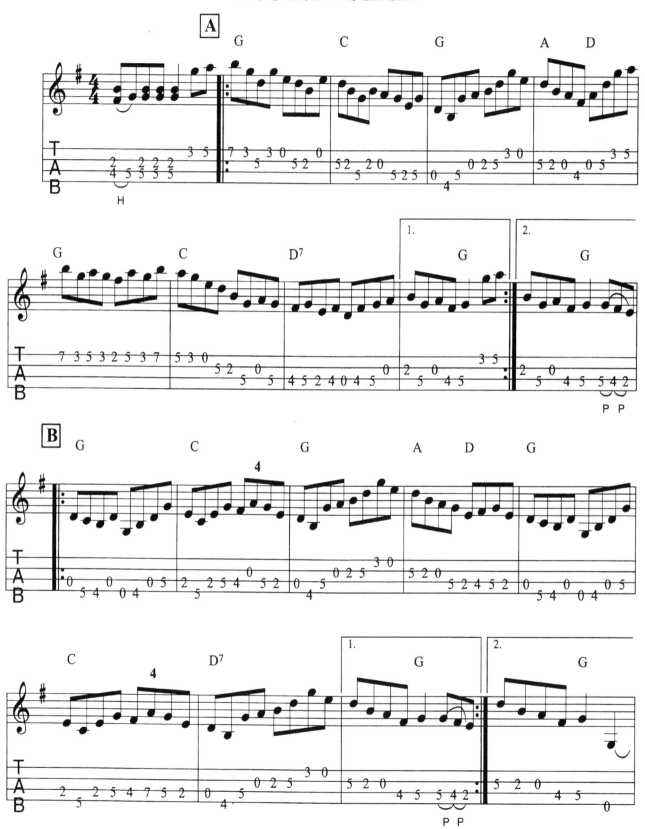

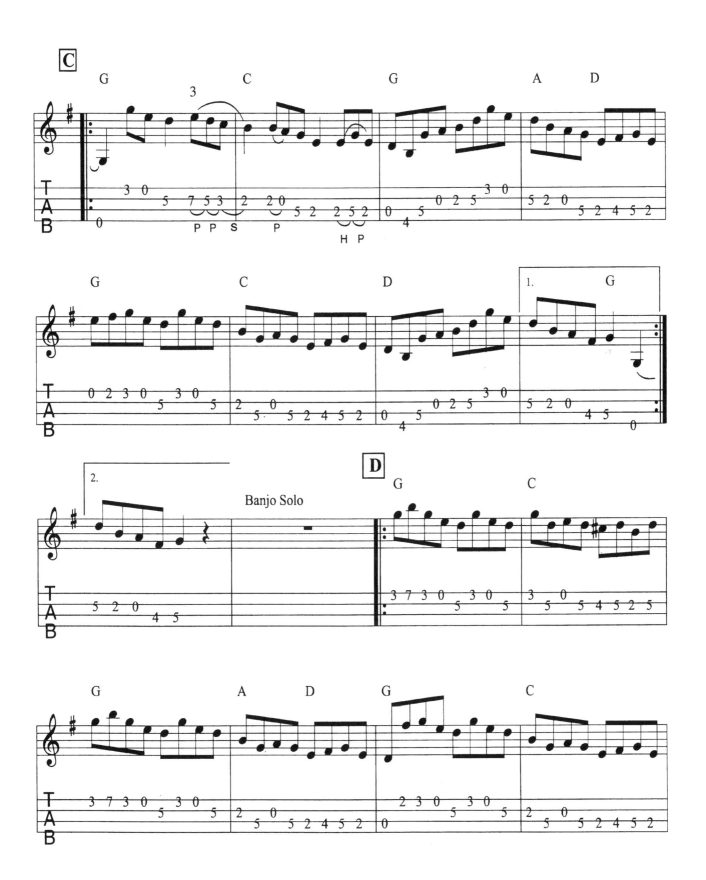

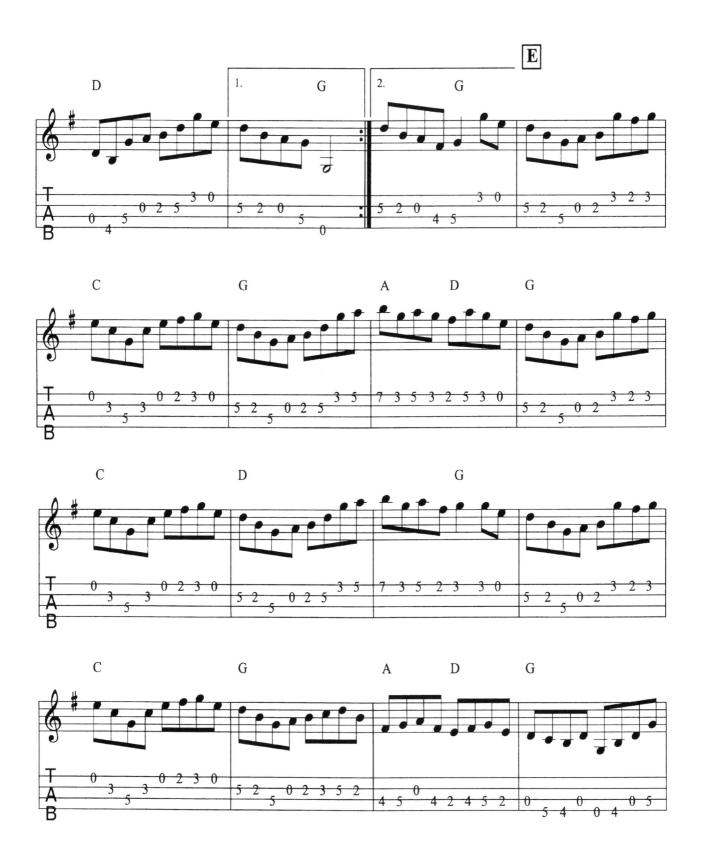

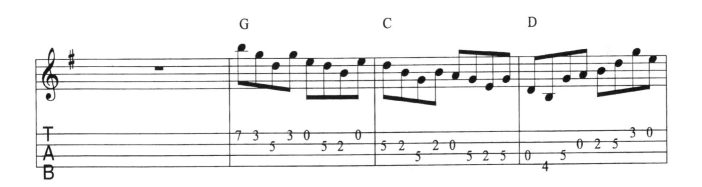

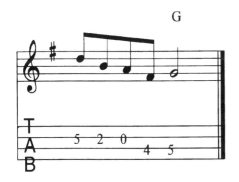

DUSTY MILLER

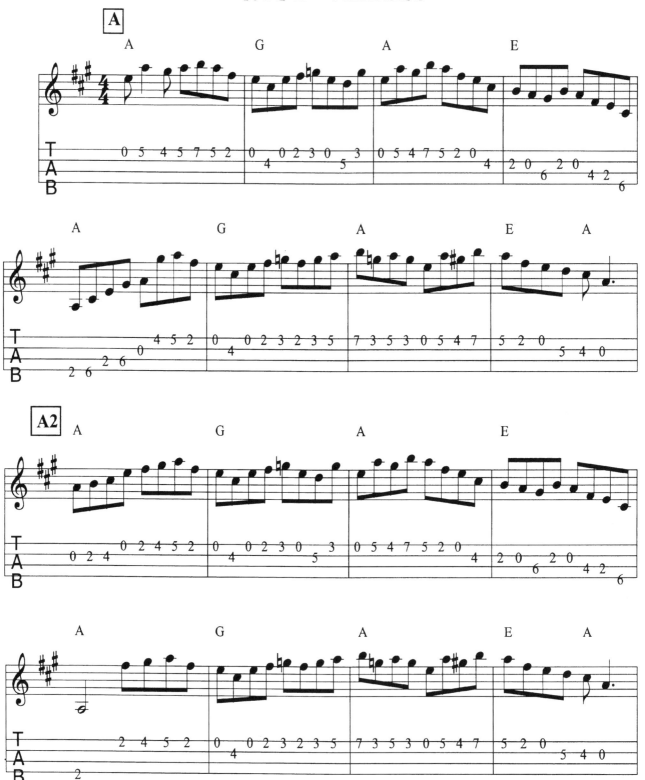

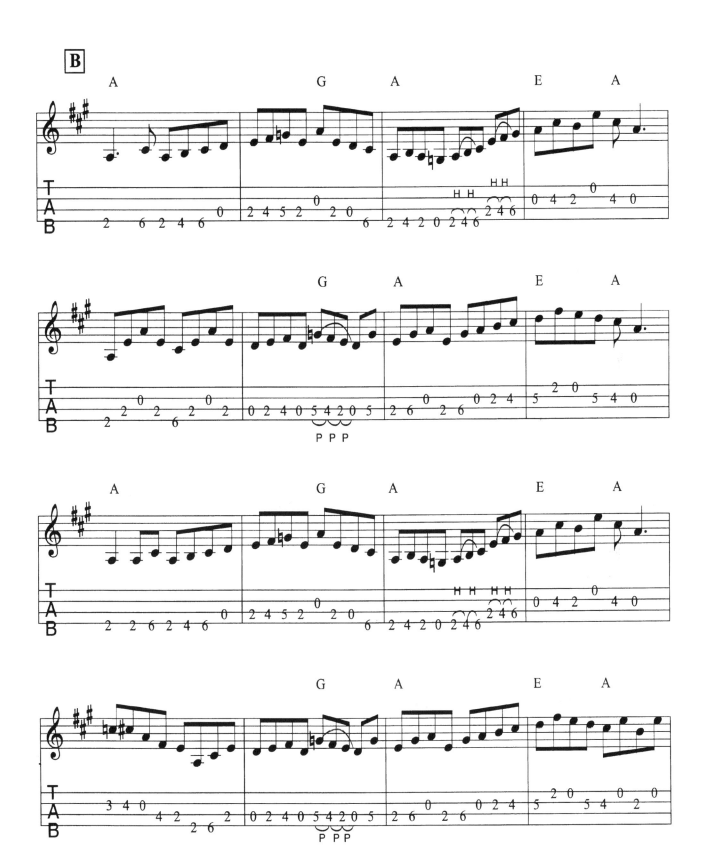

31

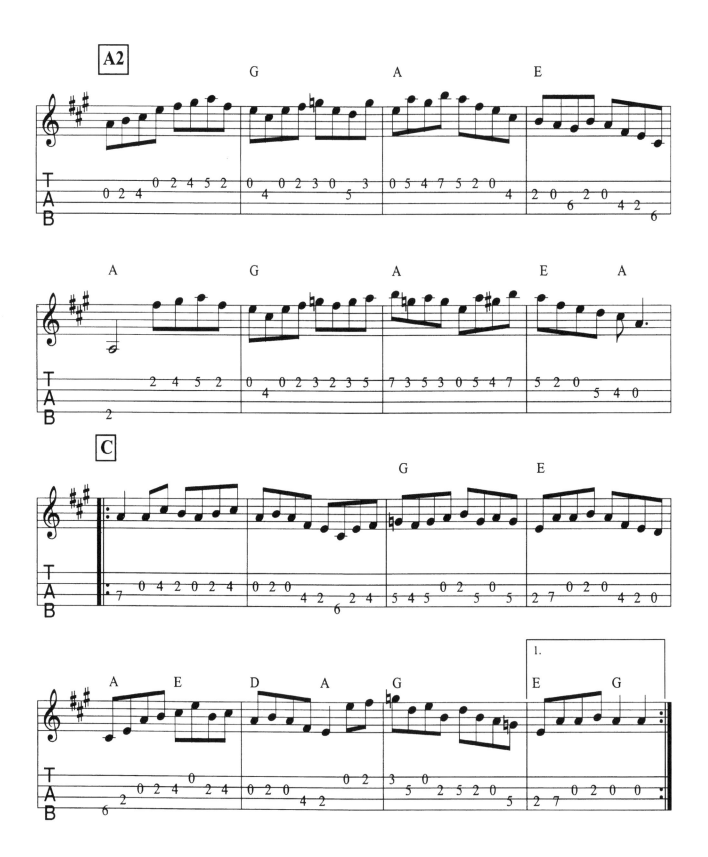

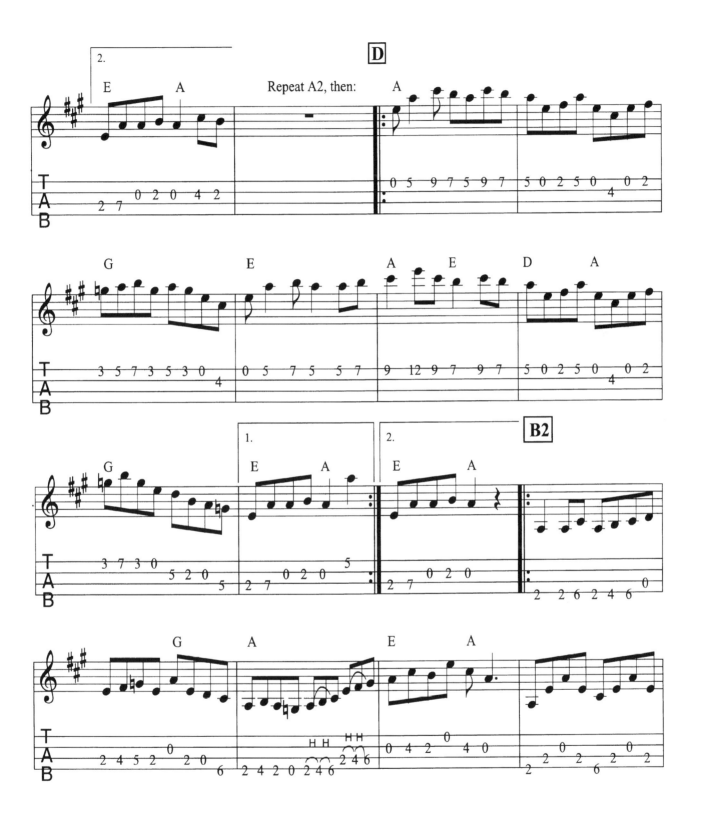

33

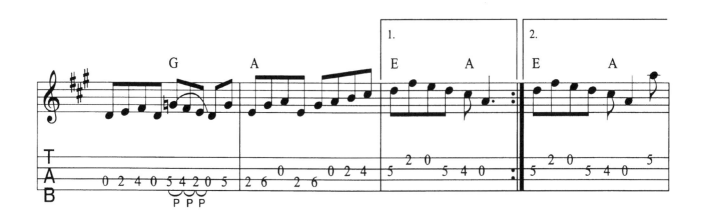

Ending

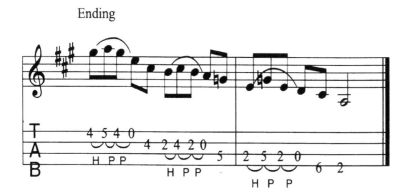

TWINKLE LITTLE STAR

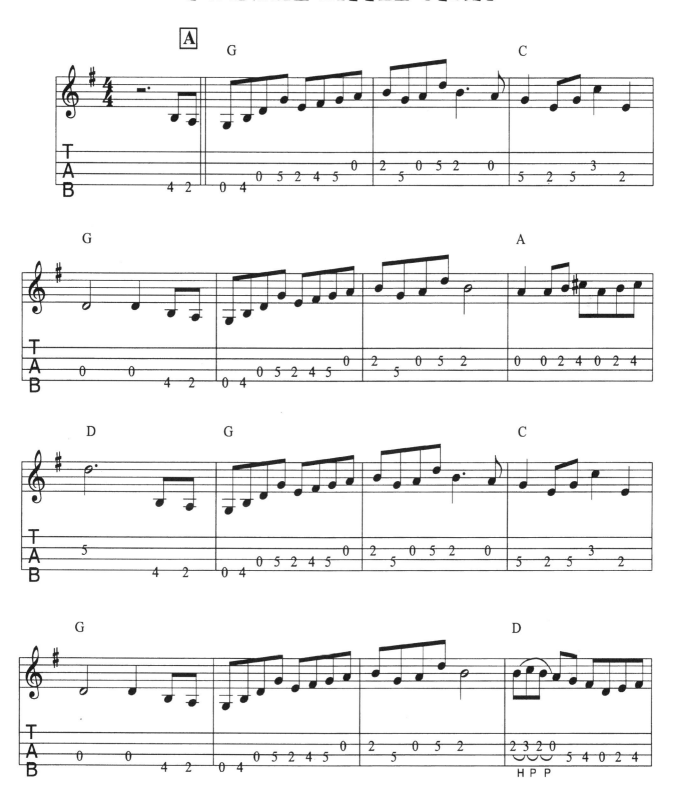

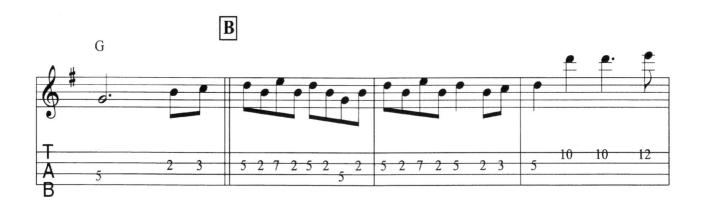

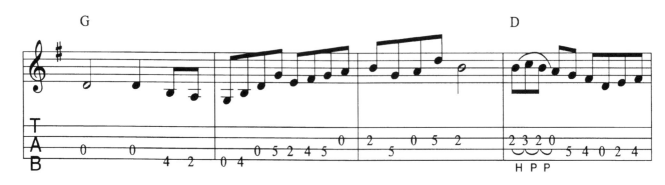

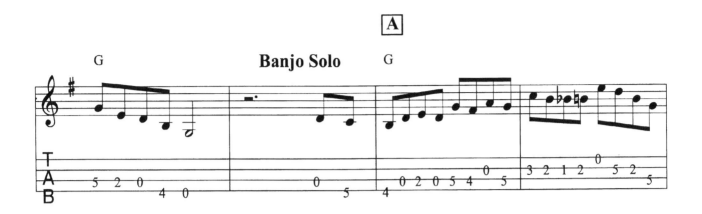

Banjo Solo

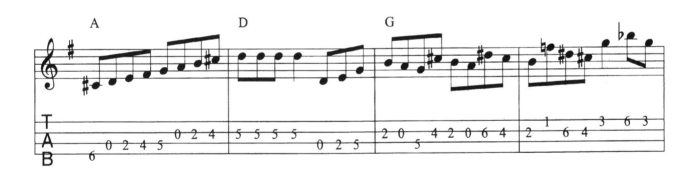

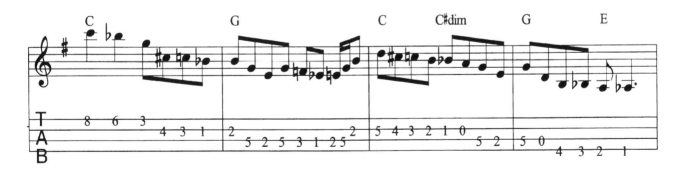

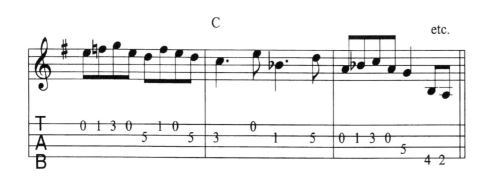

This page has been left blank to avoid awkward page turns

SOPPING THE GRAVY (LITTLE BETTY BROWN)

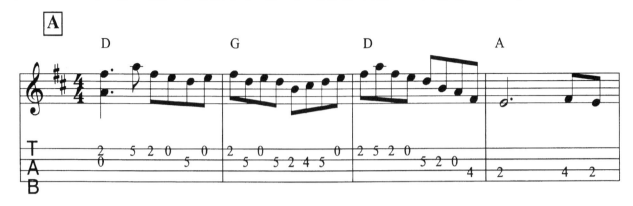

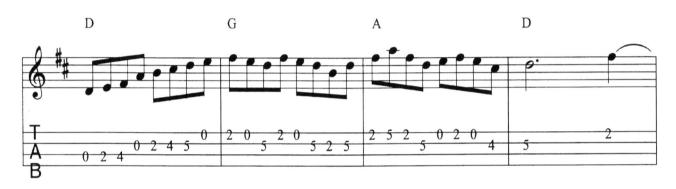

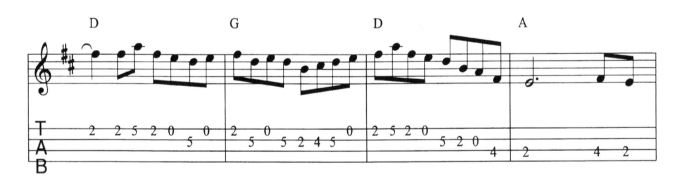

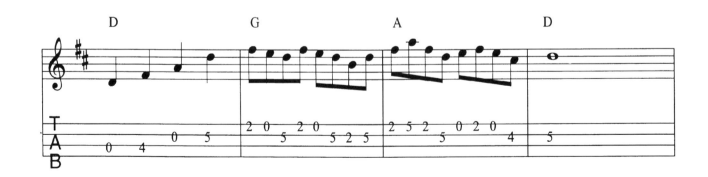

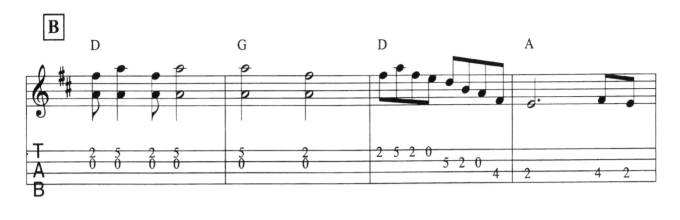

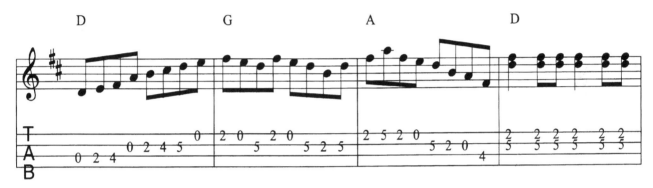

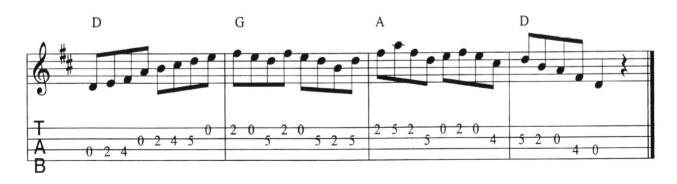

ACE OF SPADES

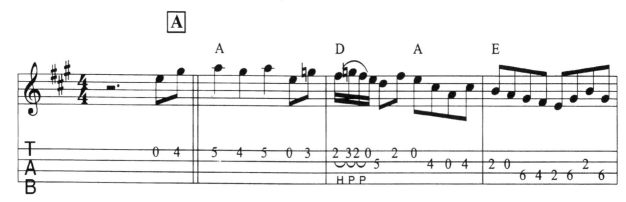

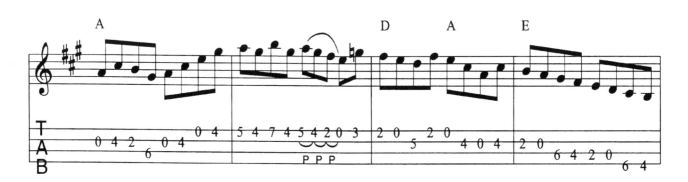

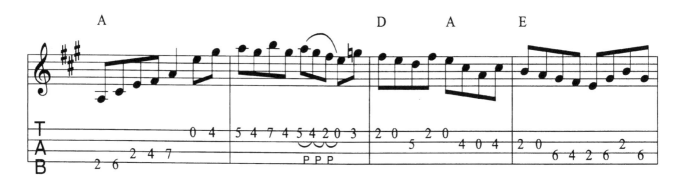

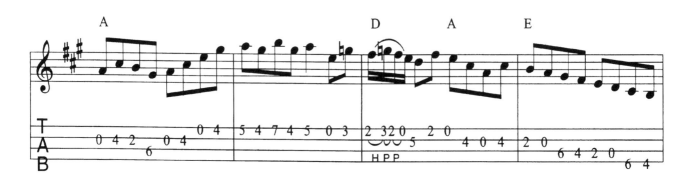

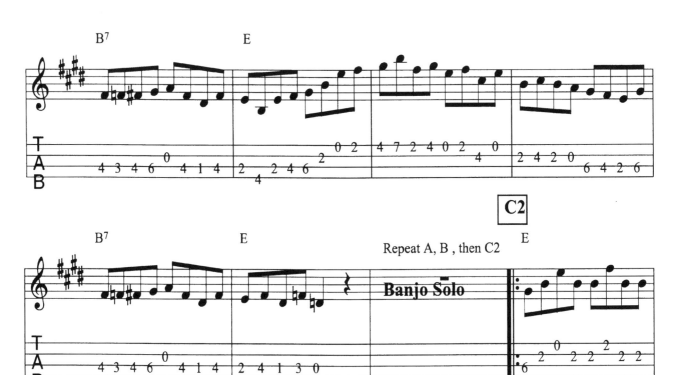

C2

Repeat A, B , then C2

Banjo Solo

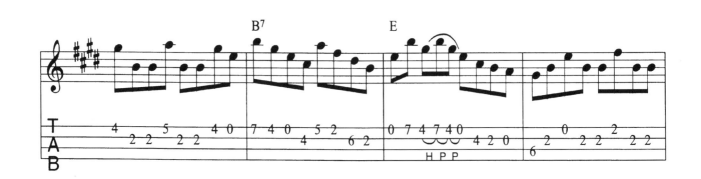

44

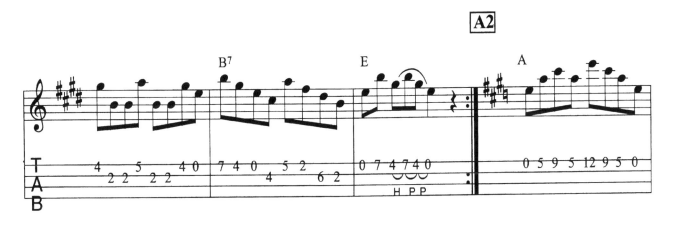

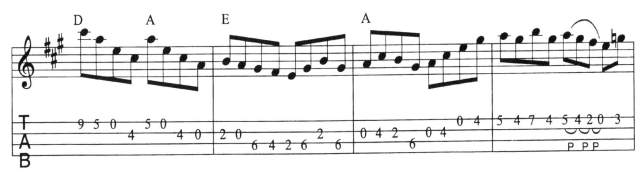

Ending

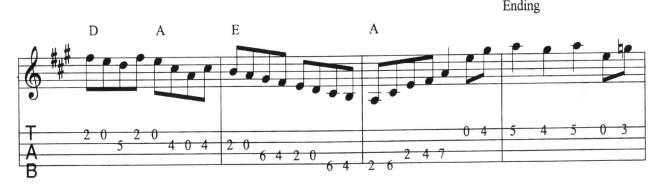

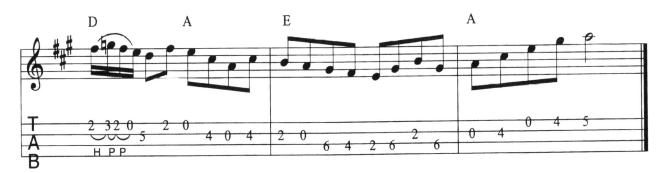

DILL PICKLE RAG

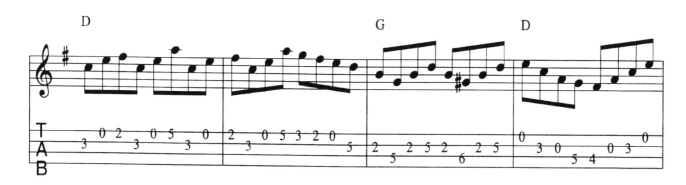

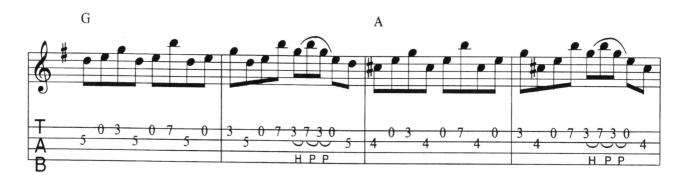

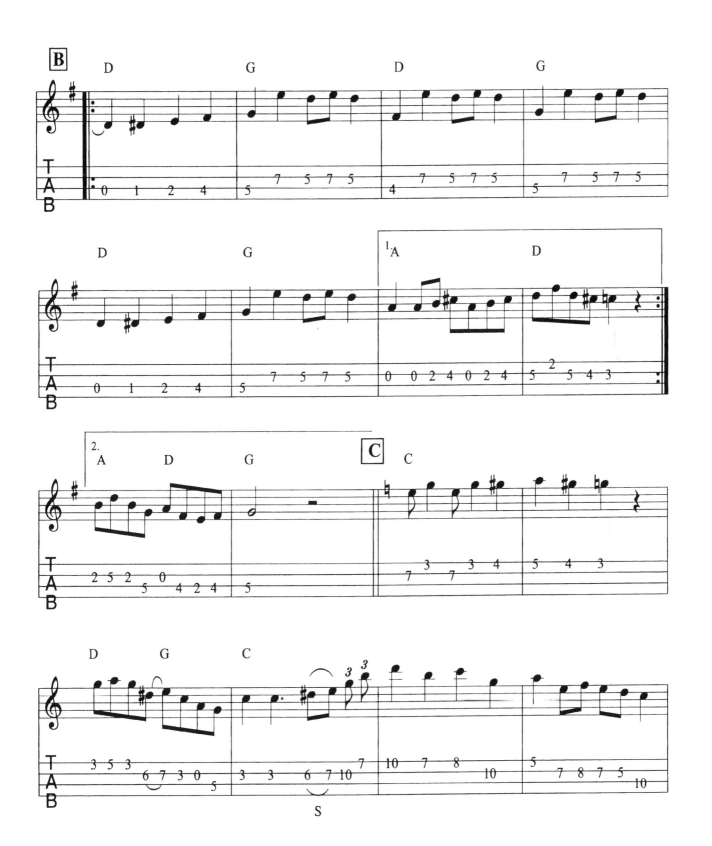

Turn page →

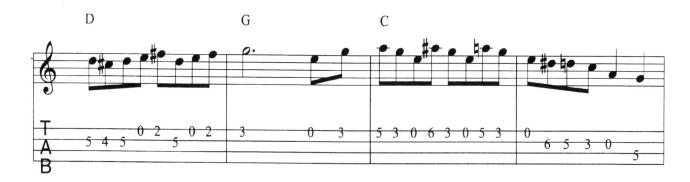

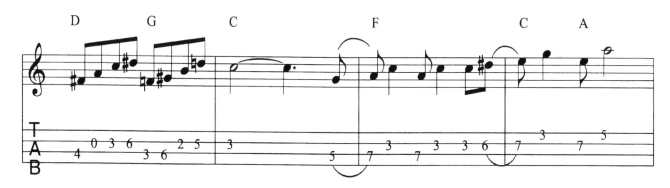

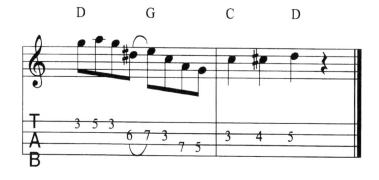

Made in United States
Troutdale, OR
03/24/2024

18711585R00029